SEARCH EVERY CORNER

SEARCH
EVERY
CORNER

SEARCH EVERY CORNER

June Parker Goldman

2373

Nashville   Abingdon Press   New York

SEARCH EVERY CORNER

ISBN 0-687-37125-2

Library of Congress Catalog Card Number: 74-186823

Scripture quotations are from the Revised Standard Version
of the Bible, copyrighted 1946 and 1952 by the Division
of Christian Education, National Council of Churches,
and are used by permission.

Lines from the poem "Time, You Old Gipsy Man" reprinted
with permission of The Macmillan Company from *Collected
Poems* by Ralph Hodgson. Copyright 1917 by The Macmillan
Company, renewed 1945 by Ralph Hodgson. Also used by permission of Mrs. Hodgson; Macmillan London & Basingstoke;
and The Macmillan Company of Canada Limited

MANUFACTURED BY THE PARTHENON PRESS AT
NASHVILLE, TENNESSEE, UNITED STATES OF AMERICA

*Dedicated with
deep affection to
my three children:*

*Candace, whose inspiration
prompted the writing of
this book*

*Jennifer, whose encouragement
kept me writing even when
I didn't feel like it*

*and
Stuart, whose persistent humor
helped me keep things
in balance*

Parenthetical Preface

Logically one should never begin to write a book when one is up all night with intestinal flu. But on the other hand, when else can one stay up all night—or feel as humble?

And so, humbly, I now transfer to paper what has been in my heart for quite some time.

Preface

New discoveries add new words to our vocabulary, continually enriching our language and expanding our sphere of knowledge. One such word is orthogenesis, a word coined by a group of zoologists to describe the irreversible development of a given characteristic to a point of no return. Animals, incapable of the human function of reasoning or of scientific intervention, are powerless to reverse a process once it is underway—even though that process, if allowed to run its course, will mean the death of the species.

This was what happened, for example, to the dinosaur, whose large body was developed, to begin with, for protection as well as for the purpose of overpowering other animals for food. Unfortunately, however, this prehistoric animal's tendency toward bigness ran away with itself (or perhaps it would be more accurate to say that it became hopelessly bogged down), and the original purpose was lost. The orthogenesis of the dinosaur's great size resulted in the inevitable extinction of that form of life.

Similarly, through this type of irreversible process, the Irish elk of the Pleistocene Age suffered its demise. It began to develop wide and powerful antlers to use as a

9

formidable weapon against its enemies. But the antlers kept growing and branching out so far that eventually the elk could no longer take refuge in the forest. Where the trees grew closest and therefore offered the greatest protection, the elk could not go. Consequently, having to remain on the edge of the forest, this species of wide-antlered elk became an easy prey for predatory animals; and it wasn't long before the entire herd disappeared.

It may not be amiss to borrow this concept of orthogenesis from the zoologist and apply it to our human condition. Could it be that man, even with his capacity to reason and to experiment, is setting in motion certain irreversible currents of thought or systems of political action or modes of morality which, if allowed to run their course unchecked, will pull him into oblivion?

On the one hand, the prophets of doom, of which there are more than enough, point frantically to the danger signs along man's present journey and urge him to step back from the precipice. On the other hand, there are the hawkers who blatantly peddle "change for the sake of change" and keep insisting that man can never "go back," that values are ephemeral, and that whatever may be lost along the way can never be regained.

It seems to me (and I hope I am not being an ostrich in this matter) that man can and must make some reaffirmations, and that these should be, not a repetition of the disappointments he has felt, but a rejuvenation of the dreams he once followed. Man must dare to reverse those decisions which would lead to his destruction; and he must once more care enough, often enough, to halt his headlong rush to oblivion. Too much of the time man formulates his image of himself as an ineffectual creature weighted down, like the dinosaur, with an enormous problem; or, like the Irish elk, caught on the horns of his own dilemma.

But, in spite of the maelstrom of negativism in which society seems to be swirling today, man needs to believe that he doesn't have to give in to the orthogenesis of despair. He needs to be reminded and reassured that there is an intrinsic shimmering quality at the core of life. He must have the buoyancy to believe that Peter Pan *can* exist in the space age, and the boldness to assert that if Peter can, then Paul can, too—and the courage to proclaim the authority and validity of Moses and David and Isaiah—and Jesus the Christ!

If man is to survive, he must search for the Center of his being; and if he is to give his children any heritage at all, beyond a purely technological one, he must take time to remember—and to remember *with* his children. In the midst of the clamor for newness, there must be a reminder of the old; for truly "the past is prologue."

Chapter
1

Part of the essence of our humanity lies in our refusal to capitulate to anything that would push us irreversibly over the brink. The faith men cling to and the laughter they share and the tears they shed are not very different today from what they were in any other age. And each generation, if it is to grow to a healthy maturity, must learn of the faith and the laughter and the tears of the generation that has groped and grappled and grown before it.

But how do we transmit humanity's heartbeat from person to person—and how can we transfuse God's love into the veins of a sick society?

We each have a heritage and a hope to bequeath to our children—and our grandchildren—or to those children whose lives touch ours in relationships other than family ties. But what kinds of gifts shall we offer to Everychild that will be genuinely meaningful and enduring? This is a recurring question for me as I look at my own children.

I have a daughter who is in high school. She is struggling with the inner rebellions which are part of the inevitable process of growing up, and it is a difficult discipline to be patient with her. And yet I take heart in the fact that through the smoke of conflict there shines the joyful buoyancy of youth.

I have another daughter, who is in college now, living and learning on the edge of the unexpected. She has survived the turmoil of the teens and is reappraising life with a new and sturdier idealism.

My son is in his early twenties and has entered a phase of his life that he had not experienced before. He is busy translating last year's "core curriculum" into the sharp reality of this year's job, and he is quickly discovering how unexpected and often frustrating are the demands that a day may bring.

Each of my children has differing talents, different strengths, and different weaknesses; yet they all share some things in common. Certainly one such common denominator is the fact that they are all searching—reaching out for a faith that will not only bring them safely to the close of this century, but carry them happily into the twenty-first.

I became acutely aware of this searching and yearning through a poem which Candace wrote when she was home from college during Christmas vacation. She wrote it very late one night soon atfer Christmas. The days of vacation had all been incredibly full, and this was the first quiet and unhurried time that any of us had been able to find. The table lamp in the living room had been turned out, and there was only candlelight and the glow of the Christmas tree lights. The stereo had just clicked off after playing the final song in the album of Christmas carols, and the room was filled with quiet and the fragrance of evergreen.

Candace sprawled out on her tummy beside the Christmas tree and lapsed into a deep reverie for what seemed like a very long time. Then suddenly she sat up and began to write on a note pad which she pulled out of a patch-pocket. She wrote intently at first, then dreamily; then there were long pauses for thinking. After awhile some of what had been written was crossed out and new words inserted between the lines.

I was anxious to know what she was writing; but, not wanting to interrupt her train of thought, I tiptoed to bed. At breakfast I inquired what it was that she had been working on so intently, and she shared with the family the poem she had written. I listened with interest, and later I read the poem over to myself. I read it again—and again and again, and in her "Corners" I found a haunting indictment of the shallowness of our lives and the ridiculous pace at which we live them.

Was there some sort of reassurance to offer as rebuttal to the lines my daughter had written? Looking into my own heart, I read the poem still another time.

CORNERS

"Would you like to try a cherry tart?" i asked.
"This market's quite exquisite!"
"C'mon!" he snapped, and frowned and
        grabbed my coat.
        He kept me moving—just like that,
        flying at his heels.

"Stop!" i pleaded.
"Please let me stay to touch this moment;
        i will not be this way again
        and i want to remember it well."

But he tugged my arm and said there wasn't time.
There were places to go and things to do
And didn't i know by now you couldn't

stop at every corner to investigate
    its shape?

Why was i so silly?
"Hurry!" he screamed,
    pulling me madly through my life.
"You have a schedule to meet.
Now quit your nonsense and
    dawdling about the years,
And follow me—
        Quickly!"

Oh, i could have shot him then.
He was moving far too fast
    and missing everything!
He didn't care that there were corners
    and marketplaces.
He only saw the street—and that just barely.
He was concentrating on
       "THE GOAL."

We had to get there right now, if not sooner.

But i didn't want to get there now.
i didn't want to get there at all.
i wanted to sniff the spices and
    sample all the tarts and
    see which way the corners faced.
Couldn't we slow down . . . . just a little?

NO! We were late already and if we didn't hurry up
    we'd never even get there.
"Good!" i cried, "then let's not bother to go!"
But he wasn't listening.
He yanked me roughly along,
        faster and faster,
To a place i didn't care about, where i didn't want to stay.

And now we're there.
And we can't get out.
And Oh!
    i wish i could have seen
        the corners . . .

16

What I have written in the remainder of this book is an effort to respond to the wistful, wrenching cry in the final line of the poem,

And Oh! i wish i could have seen
the corners . . .

To say that *everything* I have written is in response to this one line would not be accurate, for I have tried to do more than that. I have recorded for Candace and for her brother and sister those events and ideas and feelings which I have gathered up from the deepest places of my heart and which I hope they will want to weld into the very structure of their own lives. These are some of the more important things I wish I had included in the letters I have written to my children—if there had ever been time for letters like that.

I have written very personally. And yet what I have written will find parallels in every person's life—for we are all made of the same stuff, and we are all searching.

But if, in all of our searching, we are to discover what we are hoping to find, we shall have to look in the corners!

Chapter
2

"Will you accept a collect call . . . ?"

The operator's familiar words came humming over the long-distance line at one o'clock in the morning. It was a rather uncivilized hour, to be sure, but we were not particularly surprised to see the clock hands pointing to 1:00 A.M., for that had become a sort of "witching hour" for our daughter. Happily we anticipated the sound of her voice, in spite of the fact that we had only recently paid an astronomical phone bill!

There was a slight pause—and then the opening "hello." Immediately we detected a different tone in her voice. There was a tiredness, and yet, at the same time, a tremor of urgency that alerted us to the probability of an impending crisis.

The words came in a torrent: a demonstration in Washington, D.C. . . . many classmates planning to take part . . . trying to decide between her head and her heart . . . she'd been receiving "emergency training" as a medical aide all week . . . but still she wasn't absolutely sure she should go. What should she do?

Technically speaking, I guess that phone call would have had to be classified as a monologue, although, in another sense, it was a dialogue she was having with her inner self as she tried to sort out all her conflicting thoughts and feelings. Finally there was a brief pause and she asked us again what she should do. Her father and I explained that we couldn't make her decision for her, much as we may have wanted to; and then she replied that she knew that was what we'd say, but she needed to talk to us, anyway.

When we finally hung up the receiver, we didn't know what her decision would be, whether she would be going to Washington or not. The weekend that followed seemed longer to us than any weekend we had ever spent, not knowing where our daughter was or what she might be involved with.

Then on Wednesday her l-o-n-g letter arrived—eighteen pages—and we noticed it had taken three stamps to get it across the country to us!

We learned that she had decided not to go to Washington, and we could sense the ache and the tears that went into that decision. The letter explained her reasons concisely and objectively. And then, toward the end of the letter, all the warmth and softness and longing pent up inside came tumbling across the pages:

"There's so much I want to say to you—so much that I'm not sure how to say—first, that I love you very deeply, that I don't want anything to happen to you; and that I love you more because, for all the times you make mistakes, you are also in many ways very wise." (Her father and I read that last part several times!)

"I know how disappointed you are that I'm not planning to come home at the end of this school year, but I will need to stay here for my summer job. But—no matter that we are far apart—I think of you often, of all the things you are doing, and of all the things you are; and there is no closeness like that of the heart.

"And I know that in your occasional spare moments you are wondering about me, and that you must have many questions, questions that often have no words, and that perhaps I cannot answer.

"What has this year's experience been for me? It has not been easy. No, I have not had such a hard time academically; but neither is that of great importance; grades reflect little of knowledge to me. . . . Learning is so much more than a grade point. From September 9th to May 4th—a long time, but all too short. Time is going so fast. The world is running, and I only wish to walk. I must have time to see myself, to resolve what I am and what I want to be. I feel like a folded flower that someone put scotch tape around so that it would not bloom. And, like the flower, I must fight and break the tape and bloom, or I will die, and no one will ever know what my petals have to offer. Yes, I am confused and searching. There is so much I want to be, to become, to do— myself, and with others. I have many friends, but I am so alone—perhaps we all are, and perhaps in our search that is the way it must be.

"And for all the pain it is, I am glad that I am searching. In many ways I feel very wise and very strong, and yet I also feel very unclear and so weak. We have all been going through so much this year. We have been depressed—sometimes it's just knowing that we must work when we want to play; but we know that it is deeper than that, for it is always there in the background. Life is a fragmentary thing, and we must put the pieces together so that they will stick.

"So you see that I am searching, trying to figure out how to arrange the menagerie that is me. And I know that you love me and care about how my life is changing, and you must believe in me. This is an experience only I can go through. I must make the mistakes and fall, and I must pick myself up again. And while you cannot really help me, it will be enough to know that you love me and that you understand. That is what I wished to share with you. I have said it clumsily, and maybe I've made it sound deep and melodramatic. Don't worry. I'm not withering away under the weight of my guitar.

"You know, it's funny how we joke about the 'young person's search for himself'—the typical struggle of growing up—and I guess I should laugh at myself. Perhaps you are thinking, 'Well, now, we've gotten to this stage!'— like when you lose your baby teeth and your permanent ones start growing in. But this is so much more important; you know that well, because you must lay your life on the line and pick the road that you will take, and I want to take the very best one I can."

There it was—the search for a road—The Road! Surely this is the quest of every hungry heart, and I felt the pulse of my daughter's eagerness. Instinctively I wanted to run ahead of her, to smooth out the rough spots, even though I knew full well I could not. So, hopefully, perhaps we can make the journey of exploration together. We will be retracing some familiar paths, mainly because new discoveries grow out of what we already know. Or, as the old Kentucky mountaineer so aptly put it, in his own inimitable style, "Yew cain't give what yew hain't got, any more'n yew kin come back from where yew hain't been!"

So it is that each of us may need to go back to where we've been, to remember again certain events, to re-create moods and feelings whose joy and wonder may have escaped us at first—for The Road runs through the very midst of life, which is why we sometimes fail to see it.

Chapter
3

Recently I tried to be a "good scout," keeping a pair of three-year-old twins for their mother, who was called out of town on an emergency. There were many moments in the course of the afternoon when I wasn't quite sure whether she was having the emergency or I was!

Be that as it may, the experience of looking after two lively youngsters (unaccustomed as I had become) reminded me of a time when my two older children were pre-schoolers. They were both dauntless adventurers; and, much to my husband's dismay—and mine—and our parishioners' delight, they used to trot off together to explore the community. I am quite certain that during that particular period of my life I spent half my waking hours playing "Guess which way they went." Setting out from the parsonage, I must have had "that look," because, more often than not, the people I met would ask, "Are you looking for the children *again?*" I would always try to smile nonchalantly, as if I were just out for a little walk; but everyone knew that I surely didn't take *that* many walks a day!

I recall one morning in particular. I had a pie in the oven which was more than just an ordinary pie. It was a Bribe, and I was baking it to entice the children to play in our own backyard and not go wandering off. Apparently the aroma of the pie didn't begin to waft its way out to the sandbox in time, for suddenly I noticed that the children were gone. I ran outdoors and over to the edge of the garden where I peered in every direction with mounting exasperation. Fortunately I was able to spot the guilty pair, way down the gravel road that led out of town to the east. My son was riding his tricycle, pulling his sister along behind in her little red wagon.

Hurrying into the kitchen, I turned the oven down as low as possible and then started in hot pursuit. However, when I reached the gravel road, the children were nowhere in sight. But, having grown accustomed to their ability to disappear almost instantaneously, I didn't panic but continued down the gravel road.

As I came to the last house on the east edge of town, I caught sight of the tricycle and wagon by the front door —and I shuddered. The house was little more than a shack and badly in need of paint; and, worst of all, it was where the town's most disreputable old drifter lived.

Answering my urgent knock, the man opened the door and invited me in. It took a moment or two for my eyes to become adjusted to the dimness inside; but when they did, I saw to my dismay that the children were perched on the man's dingy, unmade bed. And, horror of horrors, they were eating crackers and peanut butter which, apparently, the disheveled old man had given them!

My foremost thought—no, my only thought—was to whisk my children away from that wretched place. I murmured a civil but cool "thank you" to the old man, took each child firmly by the hand, and headed quickly for the door and the purifying sunshine. But before we could get outside, our host said in a quavering voice, "Please—wait just a minute. I want to show you something."

Unable to imagine that there could be anything of interest in that pitiful shack, I tarried a moment. The old man shuffled over to a chest of drawers and took out a violin! Lifting the instrument to his shoulder, he played a surprisingly lovely melody. When he finished, I thanked him; and this time the "thank you" was more genuine.

"Guess most folks don't know I play the fiddle," he explained hesitantly, "but I've enjoyed it for years." Then, musing with a faraway look, he continued, "Lots of nights I play for hours down here—yup, just me and my fiddle and the music . . . here, let me show you this other one!" He hobbled over to the opposite corner where he lifted another violin out of a rusted metal chest.

He walked back over to us, stroking the violin lovingly. "Now this one I made myself," he announced proudly, "out of bits and pieces I picked up at the dump."

Placing the instrument in position, he played another tune for us. It was hauntingly beautiful, and the music momentarily transformed the old man's face—a face that spoke of a life that once had had many possibilities, but . . .

When he finished playing, we all stood hushed—as if someone had just offered a prayer.

The lump in my throat made it difficult to speak as we left, so I smiled my thanks. He nodded his acknowledgment and said simply, "Thank you for enjoying the thing that I love."

I have gone down many roads, but probably none more hallowed than the ones I have traveled looking for my children. And strangely enough, when I have found them

I have also found a segment of myself that I had been trying to find—without really having been aware that it was missing until I found it.

And whenever I have felt this new sense of wholeness, I have become more aware of God-in-me and God-with-me. How surprising it is that we sometimes stumble upon his presence, not on our way to the altar, but following a tricycle and a little red wagon. . . .

Chapter
4

Since reminiscing about the old violinist, I've let my thoughts wander back to another summer when the children were ten, eight, and the tag-along age of four. That was the time that the three of them conned their unsuspecting parents into taking a few steps on the Glory Road!

It was a miserable, hot July afternoon whose high humidity was mitigated only by the air of excitement that hung over the town. The carnival had arrived! And there was a frenzy of activity in the center of town where the rides and concession stands were being readied for the evening.

About midafternoon the children came running the five or six blocks from the carnival site to our house. Breathlessly, and with eyes dancing, they announced that they had invited one of the carnival couples to park their camper-trailer in our driveway and hook up to our water and electricity.

My husband and I were aghast. Carnival people parking right beside us—and not just for one night, but for *three?* It was unthinkable! We had heard a lot about carnival people, and none of it had been complimentary.

"We can't have them!" we said sternly.

"But why not?" came the obvious question.

"Because we don't know anything about them."

"But they're very nice," all three children protested, standing their ground.

Then, as if to bolster his position, our son added, "Besides, they won't be around during the day; they'll be busy at their jewelry booth. They'll be here at their camper just to sleep."

The three children looked up at us expectantly, hoping that the arguments just presented would change our minds.

"That may be so; but still, it just wouldn't look right to have carnival people parked in the parsonage driveway!" (Was that really *my* voice?)

My remark almost stopped any further discussion, but the children weren't to be daunted for long.

"But Daddy, you always preach that we should love *everybody*—and aren't carnival people part of everybody?"

This one stopped *us*. There was absolutely no rebuttal to our son's question, and we knew it. Sheepishly (and we hoped it didn't show), we admitted that our children were right; then we suggested that they go back to the carnival and direct their new friends back to our driveway.

The three children were so ecstatic their feet scarcely touched the sidewalk as they scampered off on their happy mission! To say that their father and I did not share their elation would have been an understatement. As a matter of fact, the next several minutes were filled with painful misgivings as we awaited the arrival of the people in question.

It wasn't long before the children rode triumphantly into the driveway in the camper-trailer. Caesar, returning from Gaul, could not have been as jubilant!

27

At first meeting we had to admit that the couple from the carnival appeared to be altogether respectable, and their camper was spotless! Wewere more than a little embarrassed by their obvious appreciation of the invitation to use our electrical and water outlets; and, to show this appreciation in a more tangible way, they presented each of the children with a long roll of tickets for free rides at the carnival!

After the first evening's festivities, we invited the couple over for coffee. We talked together until two o'clock in the morning! They had an intensely interesting story to tell. Because they enjoyed traveling, they had chosen to go with the carnival because they felt that they could be of special help there, acting as "proxy parents" for the many carnival children who had to shift for themselves when their own parents were too busy to look after them.

The couple shared a wide variety of experiences with us, and we were deeply touched by their concern for the way some people have to live. We could have talked together the rest of the night and still not heard all the stories that they could have told about the people and places that had become an integral part of their lives.

For three summers following, when the same carnival came to our community, this couple parked in our driveway. And, for a number of years, we exchanged Christmas greetings. Our first evening together had marked the beginning of a warm and delightful friendship—and to think we would have missed it all if we hadn't been reminded that carnival people are "part of everybody"!

We had been reminded, too, to take a look at another simple but important truth: "Unless you turn and become like children, you will never enter the kingdom of heaven."

Chapter
5

Having followed a couple of long-ago winding roads—one that led to an old shack on the edge of town and another that angled around to a carnival midway—I feel that I should retrace some steps over a road that was traveled more recently. It's one of my favorites! It was the road that our older daughter took one muddy spring day not long after her sixteenth birthday, just a few weeks after she acquired her driver's license. I smile when I think about that day; but even as I do so, I feel a catch in my throat.

She had gone out to check the picnic area at Pilot Knob Park to see whether or not the ground had dried off enough to allow her to go ahead with the wiener roast she had been planning for several of her friends. It seemed that she was gone much longer than necessary, but when she came back it was easy to understand why.

Visibly shaken, she came into the house with the sobbing announcement that she had wrecked the car. The sad shape of our family's small economy car was her over-riding concern—so much so that she was unaware that her nose was badly bruised, perhaps even broken, and that her face was swollen and bleeding.

On the way to the doctor she told us what had happened. The roads in the park had been slippery with the spring mud, and she had slid off into the ditch; but in sliding off, the car had come to an abrupt halt astride a large tree stump and she had been thrown against the windshield. Fortunately there had been some hikers nearby who helped her out of the ditch, lifting the small car back on to the road. As badly bent as the front end of the car was, she had somehow managed to drive it back to town, although getting back to our house required some advanced logistics since the car could make nothing but lefthand turns!

Recalling the touch-and-go trip back from the park, she related how, en route home, she had passed a billboard along the highway which had displayed the all-too-appropriate message, "Come to me, all who labor and are heavy-laden, and I will give you rest." Then, with her irrepressible humor surfacing through her tears, she commented wryly that it was probably fortunate that that particular billboard hadn't said, "Prepare to meet thy God!"

The X rays were taken and, to everyone's relief, there were no broken bones. The bruises and abrasions healed rather quickly, the car was repaired—and the very sizable bill was taken care of, in large part, by our insurance. But it was a source of concern to our daughter that one of the clauses in our policy required us to foot the first fifty dollars of the repair bill ourselves.

"Don't worry about that," her father and I assured her. "The important thing is that *you're* all right."

And so we thought that was the end of that. But it wasn't.

That summer our daughter launched upon a new experience, taking a job as a mother's helper in a town some hundred and twenty miles away. After she had been on the job for a couple of weeks, we received a surprise package from her. Puzzled by the fact that there was no "special occasion" involved, we opened up the wrappings with great curiosity. Inside we discovered a decorative, narrow-necked bottle that was stuffed with one-dollar and five-dollar bills! In the neck of the bottle was a tightly folded sheet of stationery which I extricated with considerable difficulty. More curious than ever, my husband and I unfolded the note and read the following message:

Dear All,

This should take care of that first $50 you had to pay on the car repairs. However, you're going to have to work for it, as it isn't so easy to get out. Also, please save the bottle. ☺

With infinite patience and the longest tweezers we could find, we finally pulled from the bottle ten neatly rolled dollar bills and eight five-dollar bills. Suddenly it occurred to us that this amount was almost her entire pay for her first two weeks of work!

Our eyes welled with tears. Truly, truly, she had traveled the second mile!

Now it's been four years since that incident, and I am not really sure that my husband and I ever fully expressed our feelings about our daughter's gift. For in our hurried conversations we seem to get caught in the revolving doors of small talk and seldom say the important things that are in our hearts.

Revolving doors serve a purpose, of course—if one knows when to step out of them. All of us have watched children, gleefully hypnotized by the circular motion, going 'round and 'round with no sense of when to call a halt. And yet many of us, even after we have "grown up" (chronologically speaking), keep on playing in revolving doors, dodging issues, avoiding responsibilities, and neglecting the generous gesture because we are so caught up in the hypnotic circle of our own motion.

Possibly it is in the area of our faith that we seem to be most guilty of waste motion. We take an idea—preferably one that has a good sound to it—and we let it go 'round and 'round in our heads. Occasionally we even go so far as to allow ourselves to move it around in a Sunday school class discussion. But to grasp one of the truths of Christ and then to step out of the revolving door with it—that's something else!

Maybe we like staying in the door because it gives us the comforting illusion of going somewhere (after all, we're moving, aren't we?), whether we're actually getting anywhere or not.

The arrival of the "money bottle" helped me pinpoint an idea with which I'd been going around in circles for a long time. This was Christ's teaching about the "second mile," and I had kept it tucked away in that level of consciousness where I keep my good intentions. The phrase had appealed to me from the very first moment I heard it; there was drama and poetry and adventure in the idea! I had liked it so well that I was quite certain I had made it a part of the central core of my faith, something I could hang on to. In fact, I had become so enamored with the idea that I had decided not to risk moving out into the world with it, for fear of losing it. But the gift that came that summer, so carefully folded into the surprise package, gave me the little shove I needed to move out of the revolving doors of my cozy creed.

Coupled with the surprise of four summers ago is the line from the letter of a year ago: ". . . I want to pick the best road I can." And now it seems ironic that our daughter should have been the one asking for direction, for she had already put up some of the signposts herself and was pointing the way for some of the rest of us. And surely in the search for The Road, one of the better roads is, indeed, the one marked The Second Mile.

Chapter
6

In remembering some of the special roads I have traveled with my children, I have come unexpectedly upon a lovely road in my own childhood that I'd almost forgotten.

When I was ten years old, my father and mother and I lived in Japan in a large metropolitan port city. We were part of an international community where my father taught school. The friends who visited in our home came from both hemispheres and spoke at least a dozen languages. The visitor who was my favorite was a large, jolly European who could speak seven languages fluently and had taught himself how to sing opera in all seven! He had a magnificent voice, but his musical talent had never expanded beyond the realm of a hobby; and it was always a source of amazement to everyone that he sang operatic arias just for his own enjoyment!

It was through this friend that we learned that the great basso, Feodor Chaliapin, was coming to Japan on a concert tour. Our family immediately sent in for tickets for the performance that was scheduled for Osaka, the locale closest to us.

On the night of the concert our family and the family of our operatic friend took the inter-urban train to the neighboring city of Osaka. We made our way to the concert hall and, hearts throbbing with excitement, we took the seats that had been assigned us about half way down in the auditorium.

The lights finally dimmed after what seemed like an interminable wait. Actually, the curtain rose exactly on time; but because we had arrived early and had been sitting so long, it seemed as if we had been waiting forever.

Chaliapin strode to stage-center, and something like an electric charge leaped across to the audience. It took no more than the opening measure of music to assure us that we could expect a superlative performance.

Chaliapin was a charismatic performer, and his audience responded with rapt adoration. His "Song of the Flea" was sheer delight; and no matter how hard I clapped, I simply couldn't make it sound like enough. Never before had I applauded anyone until my hands ached!

The audience demanded encore after encore at the close of the program, and the singer was generous. Finally, however, the last encore was sung and the final curtain rung down.

Not wanting to shatter the magic mood, we all remained awhile longer in our seats, reluctant to cross the bridge back to reality. Sensing that it would be disappointingly anti-climactic to just get up and go home, "Papa" suggested that we stop at the hotel for an after-concert snack. He had learned where Chaliapin was staying and was hopeful that by stopping at that hotel we might get another glimpse of the dynamic singer.

We were well repaid for our effort, for we had been in the hotel dining room just long enough to place our order when Chaliapin and his party of seven or eight others were ushered into the dining room and seated at a table just three away from ours!

I found it difficult to take my eyes off my newly found idol, and I certainly had no idea what I was eating. As I watched the group at Chaliapin's table, my attention was divided between the great basso and his daughter. Miss Chaliapin was an exceptionally beautiful girl, perhaps nineteen or twenty, with her titian hair braided, tiara-fashion, around her head. She was vivacious and utterly feminine, and I couldn't help thinking that she should have been cast as Queen Titania in A *Midsummer Night's Dream!*

As I sat in mute admiration, I began to think how exciting it would be to say hello to Miss Chaliapin and hear her say something to me. But just about the time I decided that I had mustered enough courage to walk over to her table, a bellhop entered the dining room and handed Miss Chaliapin a note. She smiled as she read it; then, excusing herself graciously from the others at the table, she followed the bellhop out into the foyer.

A few minutes later, Chaliapin and the rest of his party rose to go. Instinctively I knew that it would have to be now or never. So, when the famous basso passed our table, I slid off my chair and, taking the single rose from the dining table vase, handed it to him. My words squeaked out of a heart that was pounding so loudly that I was afraid Chaliapin would not be able to hear what I said.

"P-p-please," I stammered, "please give this rose to your daughter. I think she is so lovely!"

Chaliapin's sensitive face broke into a marvelous smile. He accepted the rose with a deep bow; then, in his incredibly resonant voice, inquired, "This rose is for my *daughter?* Not for *me?*" But before I could say anything, he bent way down and kissed me on my forehead.

"Mama" and "Papa" have always maintained that I didn't wash my face for a week afterward!

It was an evening I would never forget; yet there had been nothing really world-shaking about it. How very simple were the things that had showered the evening with stardust: a dish of ice cream—a rose—a kiss.

Perhaps that was the beginning of my awareness that there is a rather unique satisfaction that comes from savoring a few things fully. There was a vague stirring within me that evening, an initial recognition of the fact that it is not possible to savor anything deeply and completely unless it is first of all made simple. Our senses are bombarded with so many impressions; and when these come at us all at once, our enjoyment is fragmented and, therefore, limited.

The thoughts that were set in motion that memorable evening remained nebulous for a long time, and it was many years before I was able to recognize that there was even any pattern to my thinking. But perhaps this was just as well, for sometimes our best thoughts are the ones we haven't quite put into words.

Chapter
7

Our family lives along the Mississippi River, in the southeasternmost corner of Iowa, where the boundaries of Illinois, Missouri, and Iowa converge. We have not always lived here, and the experience of living near water is new to us. We have been finding the mood of the river to be ever-changing and the view from the high bluffs breathtaking and varied. More and more we find ourselves concurring with the person who aptly observed that anyone who ever lives along the Mississippi invariably has a love affair with the River! It hasn't taken long for this infatuation to set in.

There is, certainly, much more to the river than the view. It affords so many opportunities for learning—whether a person's interests point him toward nature study or water sports, painting or poetry, conservation or commerce. However, there is one pastime that seems to have a universal appeal, to ecologist and artist and engineer alike: and this is the pleasant diversion of watching the barges travel through Lock #19 as they move their cargo up river and down.

This lock, and the dam which adjoins it, is built across

a portion of the Mississippi River between Keokuk, Iowa, and Hamilton, Illinois. At this point in the river there used to be treacherous rapids which made boat travel impossible—and people either had to portage for a few miles or travel by horse and carriage along the riverbank—but the installation of the lock and dam changed all that.

It is a source of constant amazement (whether one is seeing it for the first time or the fiftieth) to observe how rapidly the water level in the lock can be raised or lowered to accommodate the need of the particular barge going through. The entire process takes only fifteen or twenty minutes.

One day recently my curiosity got the best of me, and I went down to ask the lockmaster some questions. I inquired how much water had to be pumped into the lock each time a boat required passage. His reply surprised me on two counts: first, he corrected me by explaining that the water wasn't "pumped" in or out, that the lock was filled or emptied by what he termed "gravity-in" and "gravity-out"; and then he went on to say that it took almost thirty-eight million gallons of water to change the level of the water every time a boat went through! I had had no idea that such an enormous volume of water was involved in this process.

Through a wide array of facts that I have been gathering since then about the lock and from having watched dozens of boats go through, I suppose that it was inevitable that my mind would draw a parallel with the events of our daily lives. Particularly as I mulled over the current emphasis on "total freedom," it seemed that there might be some merit in formulating a sort of "parable of the lock."

If the captain of a river barge were to operate on the theory that all restrictions are bad, then there would be many points along the river at which he would be powerless to proceed. Upon reaching these points, the captain must relinquish his own command briefly in order to move forward. He must willingly place his boat in the lock—a very confining space—and, for fifteen or twenty minutes, become totally dependent upon a source of power greater than his own. By giving up his freedom of movement for a little while, he gains a greater freedom; for when the gate of the lock opens, the whole river once again becomes his domain. The temporary restriction of the lock suddenly and miraculously unlocks a wider freedom!

During the demanding experience of college it seems, sometimes, as if one is hemmed in, with very little say about anything. The curriculum requirements seem too binding; the assignments cut relentlessly into one's time when one would prefer to sleep or play or, for that matter, do almost *anything* rather than study! But these very disciplines are like the pull of gravity in the lock—bringing one's life to the level it needs to be in order to move on to the next series of experiences.

However, it's not only the academic life that sets limits. Beyond the bounds of study there are other disciplines equally as rigid. Sometimes the nature of a particular discipline will slow our pace to such a degree that we find ourselves rebelling at the fact that life seems to have come to a virtual standstill. Perhaps it's an interruption or a setback that we hadn't anticipated; maybe it's the necessity of making a radical revision in our plans; or, hardest of all, we find ourselves face to face with a dream that must be deferred. The wait in the lock appears intolerable! But slowly we learn that the wait is not only helpful, but an imperative necessity.

In the life of the spirit, as in our secular seeking, it is

essentially the same: there are those moments when we resent having to relinquish the forward thrust of our own strength, trying desperately to avoid acknowledging the fact that a greater power must move us where we need to go. And yet, if "gravity-in" can move millions of gallons of water and raise a boat forty feet or more in twenty minutes, then surely God-in-us can move us out of our stubbornness and substantially raise the level of our lives.

We have heard again and again the affirmation, "I can do all things in him [Christ] who strengthens me" (Philippians 4:13); but maybe we have heard it so often that we have subconsciously tuned it out. Or perhaps we have pushed aside this bold affirmation because it seemed too rash or too old-fashioned or too naïve or too something-or-other.

And yet—to use the campus vernacular, "that's where it's at!"—the power and the glory are *there*, in the strength of Christ! He is the Lockmaster, the Enabler, who opens the gates and releases the power that undergirds and surrounds us and brings our lives to the level they have to be if we are once again to move forward toward meaning.

Chapter
8

In our search for meanings we try many roads: some zig-zag or curving, some wide and straight, others hardly more than a trail. Some of the roads we take lead us from one geographic location to another, and frequently we come to a fork in the road. The decision we make at such a turning point leads, then, to other roads which, in turn, often branch out again and bring us face to face with still other choices. These choices tumble us into the dramas of life, and they determine our friendships and our very life-style.

Usually the decisions regarding physical or external roads are relatively easy to make, but it is quite a different matter when we must deal with the choices that revolve around intellectual and spiritual pathways. Probably the roads which are the most difficult to choose and then to follow are the ones which carry us over the oftentimes uncharted wilderness of our inner lives. And it is these difficult, twisting, "inside roads" that sometimes lead us to a junction in our lives when we must ask, "Can you believe and yet feel shaky about what you believe?"

No doubt this question reflects the thought that every

seeking Christian turns over in his mind from time to time. It is the same question that was asked centuries ago by another seeker who poured out his heart in the anguished prayer-petition, "Lord, I believe; help my unbelief!" This urgent plea, found in the ninth chapter of Mark, echoes our own cry. Each of us experiences a sense of paradox in our lives, to a greater or lesser degree; and occasionally these moments of wavering affect our thinking for a very long time.

I cannot help but turn back to a time in my own life when my belief was so shaky and so shaken that I almost lost it entirely.

What happened took place in one of our parishes, early in my husband's ministry. The incident revolved around Harry, the manager of the sundries store in the little town. He was barely forty and in the prime of life, robust and exuberant and genuinely interested in everybody. The whole community loved him.

One winter afternoon, he and his wife stopped in at my husband's study. They had just come back from a clinic in a nearby city where Harry had gone for a check-up because he had been so miserable with what had seemed like an unusually stubborn cold.

After having made many very thorough tests, the doctors had told Harry that he should come home, sell his business, settle all accounts, and make out a will because he would probably have no more than six or eight months left to live. There was an inoperable malignancy at the base of his skull.

The news was shattering to everybody, and Harry's "death sentence" hung like a pall over the whole town.

But Harry wasn't one to sit down and die. He sold his business, but he didn't retire. Instead, he began to write letters of application for teaching positions that might be available in the fall. And, regularly, he went for his cobalt treatments.

In the spring he signed a contract for a mathematics position in a town about a hundred and forty miles north of where we were, and the family moved there in early summer.

Never before had I seen an entire community "pulling" so whole-heartedly for one person. We all felt that Harry just *had* to make it!

In their new community, Harry bought a house for the family; and together they planted a large vegetable garden. He kept going to the hospital periodically for treatments, and he gave the doctors permission to experiment with new drugs in their frantic race against time as they battled to shrink the malignancy.

Harry and his family drove down to our town quite often to visit old friends; and always they would worship with us, sitting in their accustomed pew.

On one or two of these visits Harry seemed better, and everyone was encouraged when he began to teach school that September.

He made it through that school year with a minimum of time off. But the following summer the number and intensity of the treatments had to be increased. And when the family came back to town for an occasional weekend visit, we could see that Harry was losing ground.

One Sunday morning in late August I was sitting in the balcony of the church, where I usually sat, so that if any of the younger children sitting up there became restless I could take them down to the nursery for their parents.

The opening hymn had been sung, and we were reading the Collect when Harry and his family walked in. Having arrived after the service began, they hadn't been able to find sufficient seating space for the five of them to sit to-

44

gether on the main level of the sanctuary, so they had come up to the balcony. The seats in the row in front of me were empty, so the family took their places there, with Harry sitting down directly in front of me.

I noticed at once how thin Harry was, the loss of weight accentuated by the fact that his hair had been completely shaved off for the treatments he was receiving. The area around the base of the skull looked badly inflamed from the frequent bombardment of the cobalt beam. My eyes seemed to be drawn to the back of Harry's neck; and, with my whole attention focused there, I became oblivious of everything else.

And then I experienced the strangest sensation in my fingers—a tingling urge to place them at the base of Harry's head. What a preposterous idea that by touching him I might heal him! I pushed the thought away because it was so startling.

What if . . . what if it *were* possible to heal him?

My hands had never felt like that before.

But then a warning light flashed across my consciousness: what if I were to place my hands on Harry and nothing happened? This was even more frightening than my first thought.

I believed that it *was* possible for one to heal another by touch, but I couldn't quite believe that *I* could do it. And if I tried—and it didn't work—I sensed how shattering it would be to my faith.

At that point in my life I was not yet sure enough, and I couldn't bring myself to risk the possibility of losing what little belief I had managed to build. And so the awful debate raged within me all through the worship service. Did I dare try what my fingers ached so to do?

Suddenly the congregation was standing for the final

hymn. The opportunity was past. And I would never know if . . .

Harry died a few days after Christmas.

For a long time I struggled with a sense of guilt, and I felt a hollowness in remembering how weak I had been. My faith, which I had been so careful to protect, became more vulnerable than it had ever been; in fact it almost withered away.

But ever so slowly came the realization that my time for a miracle might not have been that Sunday, after all. At first this thought seemed to me like a shallow exercise in rationalization. But more and more I came to feel that I really had not been ready for what I had thought I could do. It would have been as incongruous as asking a first-year piano student to play one of Rachmaninoff's piano concertos.

I turned often to that familiar passage in the Book of Ecclesiastes which reminded me that "to everything there is a season." But my greatest reassurance came from two of Paul's letters. In writing to the Hebrews, particularly to those among them who were immature and insecure in their faith, he said: "For though by this time you ought to be teachers, you need some one to teach you again the first principles of God's word. You need milk, not solid food; for every one who lives on milk is unskilled in the word of righteousness, for he is a child. But solid food is for the mature, for those who have their faculties trained by practice to distinguish good from evil." (Hebrews 5:12-14)

Supplementing this idea, but introducing a further thought, Paul wrote in another of his letters the following helpful suggestion: "It is best for you now to complete what a year ago you began not only to do but to desire, so that your readiness in desiring it may be matched by your completing it out of what you have." (II Corinthians 8:10-11)

Perhaps in trying to determine whether or not it is possible to believe but to be shaky in that belief, we need to keep in mind the important distinction between having one's faith shaken and having it toppled.

Shaking something results in a realignment, a regrouping, a restructuring; whereas toppling means capitulation.

A certain amount of shaking up can be beneficial—just as exercising the body improves muscle tone and circulation and sets our blood coursing more vigorously through our bodies, restoring the glow of health. In similar fashion an experience that shakes our faith makes us re-examine our creed; it awakens us from a passive acceptance of the platitudes that have, perhaps, made us feel too comfortable; and it puts a new vitality into the ways we witness.

Could it be that sometimes, when we begin to feel that wavering of the spirit, we might think of it as a signal that God is putting through a Person-to-person call to us?

Chapter
9

Too often, hurried into taking short cuts in our thinking, we relegate all healing to the realm of the physical. When we hear such a phrase as the "miracle of healing," we instinctively think that this refers to the restoration of physical health. But the miracles of healing take place in other areas of life. And another thing that is difficult to keep in mind is that a miracle doesn't necessarily have to be an all-at-once kind of thing in order to be a miracle!

We are an impatient lot; and in our push-button environment we have become accustomed to thinking that our actions should produce results immediately, if not sooner. But life refuses to be stampeded, and there are many things which must lie dormant for a season before there is a stirring.

I was visiting recently with a retired schoolteacher who told me a rather remarkable story that grew out of her early years of teaching. It made such an impact upon me that I feel I should share it with others.

In this woman's first year of kindergarten teaching, she had a little boy in her class who was very repugnant to her. He was dirty, his clothes were ill-fitting and ill-smelling, and he seemed to have an abnormally large head. Although she knew she was being remiss in her duty, she could not bring herself to get any closer to Howie than necessary.

One morning she was supervising recess when suddenly she saw Howie running toward her with several boys in hot pursuit. He flung himself against his teacher for protection, and instinctively she threw her arms around the frightened, sobbing boy. In pulling him close to her, she discovered that Howie's head wasn't malformed and abnormally large as she had always thought. Rather, the little boy's hair was so thick and so matted with dirt that it stuck out all over, giving the illusion that the head was misshapen.

Realizing the frightful condition of the little boy's hair, the teacher decided that something should be done. She sent a carefully worded note home to Howie's mother, asking permission—in as diplomatic a way as possible— to give her child a shampoo.

The next morning Howie brought a note from his mother. It was scrawled on a piece of brown wrapping paper, and there was just one brief sentence: "Do anything you damn please!"

The teacher knew then, beyond any doubt, that Howie needed help. So she arranged with the school custodian to use his washroom facilities to give Howie a shower and shampoo the following morning. She also asked a friend of hers, whose son was in the first grade, if she could have some of his outgrown clothes.

The next morning when Howie arrived at school, the teacher saw to it that he had a shower and shampoo; then she gave him a clean and attractive outfit to wear. The transformation was incredible!

When it was time for Howie to go home that day, the

teacher suggested that he change back into his own clothes.

The next day the process was repeated. Howie had his shower and shampoo and changed into a fresh set of clothes. Every morning afterward this became a part of Howie's regular routine.

The teacher didn't terminate her special project after a few days or even after just a few weeks. Every day and every day she came early to school—all fall, all winter, and into April; and every day Howie had his shower and shampoo and some clean clothes to wear; and every day he warmed to the love and pride in his teacher's eyes.

Then, in mid-April, Howie's family moved to the Southwest and the teacher lost track of them.

Many years passed, almost twenty, and the teacher was living in a town some fifty miles from where she had first started teaching. One Sunday afternoon she answered her doorbell and found two handsome Air Force officers at the entrance. One of them stepped forward and grinned broadly, "Do you remember me?"

The teacher looked at the shock of curly auburn hair that fell across the soldier's brow when he raised his hat—and then, seeing the deep dimple in his chin, she knew, even after so many years—"Howie!"

She invited the two young men in to visit over coffee, and they talked and talked for well over an hour! In the course of the conversation the teacher learned that, not long after Howie's family had moved to their new location, his father had been sentenced to life imprisonment at the state penitentiary. Two years later Howie's mother had died of delirium tremens. And then, adding further tragedy to the family's staggering list of misfortunes, Howie's brother and sister had both been committed, in their middle teens, to a mental institution.

And yet, in spite of everything, here was Howie—First Lieutenant in the United States Air Force—who had traveled many miles out of his way that day to find his very first teacher so that he could say to her, "Thank you for loving me in kindergarten!"

My throat ached with tears as the teacher finished her story, and I could see that there were tears glistening in her eyes as she leaned back in her chair and smiled.

"There have been many rewarding experiences that have come from my long years of teaching," she said softly, "but even if there had been no other satisfactions, Howie alone would have made all the years worthwhile!"

Sometimes it takes a long, long time to measure a moment—or a man. As my daughter wrote in her letter from school after that turbulent weekend with which she had had to come to grips, "Time is going so fast and the world is running, and I only wish to walk." I covet for her the continuing wish to walk. We miss so much when we run, and the roads most worth traveling are the ones which hold such wonder and joy that we have to *walk* them!

Chapter
10

Errands sometimes take us on roads we've never used before. So it was that I was driving home one day from a farm home at the farthest end of our parish; and, along the way, I saw something so astonishing that I pulled the car over to the side of the road and watched for awhile.

It had been frightfully hot for several days, and that morning the thermometer by our back door had been registering in the high nineties since ten o'clock. There wasn't even a whisper of a breeze to relieve the suffocating heat.

It was just noon as I drove by a wire-fenced field where a horse and her colt had been put out to graze. There wasn't a single tree or rock or building in that field— nothing to create any shade for the two animals there; and the sun was merciless.

As I observed the scene, suddenly I realized why the mother horse was standing where she was. Her colt was lying down, and the mother had positioned herself at such an angle as would create a shadow in which the colt could lie, protected from the blazing sun. The mother horse stood perfectly motionless, with the blistering noon sun beating down on her back, her body providing the only patch of shade in the entire field!

When you see something like this, it becomes entirely natural to think in parables; in fact, it is difficult to think in any other way! And so, as I drove back to town, I thought a great deal about the beautiful tableau I had seen and the comparisons it offered: the mother horse representing the church, and the colt the younger generation as it struggles for life and identity.

The church has frequently borne the blistering attacks of its critics (even the hot anger of the very ones whose life she is trying to protect and nurture). And yet she continues to stand, in the glare of ridicule and the hot new wave of rebellion, guarding the life of each new generation entrusted to her care. And frequently the young, like the colt, lie safe in the shade, unaware that the protective coolness has been provided at great cost.

But I am being unfair and too harsh. It is certainly not just the younger generation that plays the colt. Most of us, whatever our age, have to a great extent accepted freely all the benefits of our faith and all the sacrifices of the church without much concern for the Body that has borne the terrible heat for us.

I have been having many misgivings about my own weak discipleship, and I find myself echoing many of my children's questions—even though I am more than twice their age! But I keep telling myself (and I hope very much that it isn't just a fancied-up piece of rationalization)—I keep telling myself that this continuing questioning has its good points, too, like the benefit gained by a plant when the soil around it is loosened periodically to allow the air and moisture to reach the roots more easily. In similar fashion, when our mind-set becomes tightly packed down, as it sometimes does, the ground of our faith needs to be turned over for exposure to the restorative alchemy of fresh insights and a deepened awareness.

Much like the impact of the pastoral scene of horse and colt was the experience I had one Lenten season when I stepped into a neighboring church. In the chancel area, to one side of the altar, a crude cross had been erected by lashing two saplings together. Nailed on the cross-arm of this rustic cross was a strip of unevenly torn white cloth on which had been scrawled the question, "Is it nothing to you?"

I stood for a long time in that quiet sanctuary trying to answer that searing question. The anguish of the shattered body—and the shattered hope—was this nothing to me? Did I, by the way I was living—or not living—negate the validity of The Gift?

And, stopping by that sun-scorched field, the same question burned into my consciousness. I can only hope that it will continue burning—not the way a smudge pot does, but as a clear, bright flame.

Chapter
11

How fortunate it is that sometimes the road leads to the attic! For sorting through attic accumulations is like finding buried treasure! And that is precisely what I discovered when I tackled the long-postponed task of unpacking some boxes which I had preferred to forget were there, and came across the small piece of quilt that goes way back to the Revolutionary War and holds so much of our family's history in it.

It was just before the battle at Groton, Connecticut, that the quilt began its long journey into our household. My own great-great grandmother, learning of the approaching Redcoats, wrapped the family silver in her best quilt and hid it in the deep woods that bordered her home. Her husband was killed in the battle that ensued, and the young wife was left alone with a family to raise.

She retrieved the quilt and sold the family silver. The money she received for the beautiful silver pieces helped her get a foothold as she set about the difficult task of rearing the children by herself. With tremendous energy and resourcefulness she was able to bring all the children safely to adulthood. And because she wanted them to remember what it was that had contributed, initially, to their well-being, she divided the quilt evenly and gave each of the children a section of it at the time of their marriage.

Years passed, and as the next generation of children arrived and grew up and married, they also received a piece of the original quilt. These pieces, in turn, were divided again and passed on to the children in the next generation.

So, eventually, a very much smaller section of the quilt reached me. The piece that I have is just big enough to be divided once more, and each of my children will be able to have a small segment of this historic quilt. Because it wouldn't be practical to divide their pieces into any smaller strips, I think I shall frame each piece, together with the story of the Battle of Groton and their great-great-great grandmother's hidden silver. These bits of quilt have no monetary value, to be sure, but the story behind them is of infinite value, at least to our own family.

Sometimes an object that has been in a family for a long time becomes an heirloom; other times it is a special family tradition that gradually attains the status of an heirloom; and occasionally even a letter will find its way into the heart of a family.

I have such a letter, one that I've treasured for more years than I care to admit. It was written to me when I was a college sophomore; and when it came, it really saved the day! Apparently I had gone into a slump halfway through my second semester; and my father, sensing the uneasiness and depression I felt, wrote one of his happy, reassuring letters which invariably managed to turn me right side up. This particular letter was somehow "special," ending as it did with some wonderfully practical suggestions, written partly with tongue in cheek.

I kept the letter, feeling sure that there would be other

places along my road where there was a bridge out. Gradually, as I've read and re-read the final paragraphs of the letter over the years, their homespun philosophy has worked its way so completely into the very fabric of my own thinking that it is now almost impossible to distinguish where Papa's thoughts end and mine begin.

I've thought of making a copy of it for each of my children so they'll have it as a handy reference when they hit their sophomore slump or the senior shakes or the job jitters. Their grandfather's letter would surely qualify as an heirloom—not a very conventional one, to be sure, but an heirloom in the best sense of the word, as the excerpt that follows will testify:

". . . I hope you took the weekend off and had a fine rest and now feel more like tackling your work. Don't let your assignments get you down. Just keep at 'em. But don't work till midnight more than once a week. *It doesn't pay.* You are tired the next day and can't do good work. Get to bed at a sensible hour; in the end it will pay. Keep up your exercise, too: a fresh mind in a fresh body will get you across all the low spots.

"Incidentally, don't let others' gripes influence you. In every group there is bound to be a griping section. Don't listen to them. Stick to the cheering section.

"The art of thinking clearly and optimistically involves the ability to keep all the strands of thought from getting all tangled up. If you keep each worry, each problem absolutely separate, then it is much easier to solve the problem or dispose of the worry. Bunch your happiness but don't bunch your worries. There's nothing like a bunch of worries to get you down. If you learn to keep all the different elements of your thinking separate, you will find that nine tenths of your problems disappear. For example, suppose you have the following worries:

1. No letter from Bob for two weeks.
2. Only C on the composition for which you were expecting at least a B.
3. Only thirty cents left until next allowance.
4. A hole in your last pair of nylons.
5. A teacher's unkind comment.
6. Brush-off by a good-looking boy at the last dance.
7. Ten thousand pages to read by next week.
8. A pimple on your nose.
9. The new dress you need.
10. A dreary letter from some Gloom Queen back home.
11. Some old and unpleasant memory.
12. Some religious or philosophical doubt.
13. Inability to choose between two or three conflicting dates.
14. No check from "Papa."
15. A depressing headline in the newspaper.
16. Two depressing headlines in the newspaper.
17. A complicated problem in French idioms.
18. Your weight.

"There—that is one worry for each of your eighteen years. Each one, taken by itself, is easily resolved; but if you mix up all eighteen while in a pessimistic mood, you can see that you have some pretty indigestible hash. Yet most people, most of the time, mix all their worries up, instead of keeping them separate, and they go on feeling very, very depressed, discouraged, disheartened, dispirited, dejected, deflated, dismal, dismayed, and all the other d_____ things; whereas if they dealt with each worry one at a time, they'd soon feel on top of the world again!"

It might be appropriate to add here the further assurance of the familiar words, "Therefore do not be anxious about tomorrow, for tomorrow will be anxious for itself.

Let the day's own trouble be sufficient for the day."
(Matthew 6:34)

Surely, now, bolstered with the story of my great-great grandmother's quilt and my father's letter and the words of the Master Teacher, I should be able to start down any road, undaunted!

Chapter
12

In many parts of the country, people (young people, especially) are taking the road that winds its way back to Galilee and the Judean hills. The new "Jesus Movement" has been coming to the forefront within the past year or so, and one cannot help wondering if its emergence can be attributed to the need for providing answers for the bewilderment and apparent purposelessness that grips so many people today. Or, conversely, is this movement posing more questions than it answers?

I suppose the only fair way to arrive at an understanding of the new movement would be to study it in the different geographical areas where it has appeared and where it is gathering momentum. Obviously there are many variations in the ways in which this new religious trend is finding expression. Basically, though, I think the movement has evolved out of a hunger to *experience* the mystical Jesus oneself instead of having to be content with a description of him, given by someone else.

The questions that my children and my friends have raised are challenging, indeed; and although I feel too inadequately informed to offer any very satisfying answers, I am grateful for their questions, because these have stirred up some other thoughts which are related, but on a tangent. However, these other thoughts might afford a base of operations from which to make some forays into an understanding of the currently popular movement toward the mystical experience.

I suppose every person wonders, from time to time, what Jesus really looked like. The question comes up quite often in the various groups with whom I work in the church; and it was raised again just recently when I showed the book, *Each With His Own Brush*, to the members of the Youth Fellowship. The collection of pictures showed the infinite variety that can be found in the interpretations of how Christ might have looked. It is probably a stroke of great good fortune that photography was an unknown art in the days when the Galilean strode through the Judean hills. Somehow something is lost when we delineate our heroes too sharply.

Perhaps this is why I find the film portrayals of the life of Christ so unsatisfying; for each of us, in formulating our portrait of Christ, brings to that portrait all our personal needs and hopes. Only on the canvas of our own lives can Christ take on the lines and colors that will be meaningful to us.

Only once did I see a movie characterization that touched me deeply, and this was an oblique portrayal which never showed the face of Christ throughout the entire film! Instead, we "saw" Christ through the faces of the people around him, whose lives were suddenly changed by the impact of his presence.

This tremendous impact was most movingly felt in one scene in particular. A sadistic slavemaster was herding a group of galley slaves on a forced march to the coast where they were to be assigned to their ship. The journey had been long and difficult, and the slaves were almost crazed with thirst. They stopped at a small village on the edge of the desert area, and there the men were allowed to stop briefly to rest and to get water from the village well. However, one slave, who had fallen into disfavor with the slavemaster, was forbidden to have any water; and the agony in his face spoke of his desperate need for a drink.

The camera shifts its focus to a man, clad in a rough white garment, leaning over the well to draw a dipperful of water. Slowly but resolutely the white-robed figure, with his back to the camera, approaches the thirst-crazed slave who is lying in utter exhaustion and despair in the dust. Bending over the man, the Stranger gently lifts the slave's head and puts the dipper to the dry, cracked lips.

Suddenly there is an angry shout from the slavemaster who has caught sight of this gesture of compassion in defiance of his order. He advances menacingly with his short leather whip raised to punish either the slave or his benefactor—or both.

The Stranger rises slowly and deliberately and takes his place between the slavemaster and the helpless slave on the ground. The two men confront each other. Not a word is spoken by the Stranger in white, whose back remains to the camera; and although he says nothing, there is such an aura of strength and authority in his very presence that the slavemaster stops dead in his tracks. The hatred in his face turns to bewilderment, and he looks uncertainly around him. His arm which, a moment before, had been raised to strike, falls limply by his side. Then he takes a few steps backward, retreating from the steady, searching gaze of the One who has defied him. The bewilderment on his face changes to fear, and then astonishment—and he turns away, unable to face the Presence.

In this dramatic encounter we sense the compelling quality of the Master, conveyed unforgettably through the reactions of a man whose entire life-pattern is reversed by the power of the Presence.

I saw this movie several years ago, but that scene by the village well is etched indelibly on my memory. It was the one time that I felt the movie-makers had accurately captured and conveyed the charisma of Christ. To have seen his face in this scene would have weakened the deeply poignant moment. The almost unbearable intensity of the scene was possible because each person in the audience had the opportunity of *feeling* Christ instead of merely seeing him.

It becomes increasingly difficult, in the very pragmatic technological age in which we live, to convey the idea that it is neither necessary nor relevant to be able to list Christ's "vital statistics." How tall he was has little bearing on the heights to which he raised men's lives. What he may have weighed matters not at all; what does matter is the weight he carried in effecting changes in the corrupt systems of his day—and the weight his word still carries in pushing aside the "sacred cows" of *our* day! The color of his eyes changed nothing around him, but their penetrating insight into the urgent needs of the human heart opened up a new frontier of hope. Whether his chin had a beard or not is immaterial; it was the set of that chin that changed the history of mankind!

"Sir, we would see Jesus," was the eager request of many of the people living in his day. So, too, do we express this wish to see him; and no doubt this is one of the common concerns of the various Jesus movements—the attempt to find the Master, to "see" him, to experience him.

Being able to see him is only half the picture; being able to *see the change he makes in us* is the other half of the portrait. And it is a lifelong assignment to put the picture together, each with our own brush.

Chapter
13

One of the most unusual paths I ever walked along was in the Botanic Gardens in Brooklyn, New York, in that section of the gardens which has been set aside as a "Fragrance Garden for the Blind." This is a place that began as a rather nebulous dream in someone's mind, soon after the turn of this century, but grew from the dream to a magnificent reality and a very unique blessing. I had never seen anything like it before, and I was only sorry that I made the discovery of this garden just a short time before I was to leave the area. But I hope there will be an opportunity someday to retrace my steps there and take as long as I wish, lingering over the lush growth of foliage and blossoms.

At the entrance to this special area there are two large plaques, one in English script and the other in Braille, each giving the background history of this unusual garden. The inscription closes with the suggestion that the visitor take sufficient time to walk *slowly*, to rub the leaves and petals gently, and to breathe deeply of the fragrance of the blossoms.

In front of each different type of plant there are two

small plaques—again, one in script for the sighted and the other in Braille. These tell the visitor something about the plant: its distinguishing features and its various uses, particularly in the case of the herbs. I couldn't help but notice how worn the Braille letters were from the thousands of hands, over the years, that had eagerly traced over them.

As I made my way around this lovely garden for the blind, I had the strangest feeling that although many of the plants there were familiar to me, I was actually seeing them for the first time! Puzzled by this phenomenon, I finally concluded that perhaps the difference lay in the fact that I was *experiencing* the flowers instead of merely looking at them.

Feeling the variety of leaf textures and petal surfaces and lingering over the delicate fragrances, I was doing far more than I'd ever done before. Always, in looking at flowers, I had stood at a distance and admired them impersonally; but now I was touching them as friends!

Perhaps this is something we need to do with people, too. Everywhere we look we see people; and because there are so many of them, or because we are too chary of our time, we prefer not to become involved with them. So, although we are vaguely aware of one another, our hearts never touch.

No doubt my daughter's experience of this aloofness prompted her to write what she did in her letter: "I feel like a folded flower that someone put scotch tape around . . ."

It requires time to develop friendships in the quiet neighborhood of the heart, time to let the petals of one's own life unfold, and time to enjoy the flower that someone else is offering. And, sadly, nothing is at more of a premium today than time. So the buds remain tightly curled, with their fragrance locked inside them.

We may have an abundance of just about everything else—except time; and on that commodity we are short-changed more often than not. Wistfully the poet Ralph Hodgson expressed the universal longing for more time than we have for those things that we really want to do.

> Time, you old gipsy man,
> Will you not stay,
> Put up your caravan
> Just for one day?

When measured against our total life and our ultimate goals, it seems ridiculous that we should begrudge the moments we are called upon to spend, moments which would bring us closer to those very goals. Too often we shrug our shoulders and say, "But I haven't got the time right now," unaware that we shall have even less of it tomorrow.

There's not a great quantity of time for anybody anymore; so perhaps we need to concentrate on "quality control," following the lead of today's successful industrialists who operate on the imperative that the maximum mileage must be realized from every sixty minutes.

However, impressed as I may be with the efficiency of the technicians and motion-study experts, I still keep turning back to the practicality and the possibilities inherent in the teachings of Christ which he offered to us long before the era of "time studies." Life in his day may have moved at a more leisurely pace, but he was quick to recognize the frustration that people felt in their mistaken notion that a day, merely by being full, would automatically be meaningful.

And so he offered an option—a new Way that promised

fullness without busy-ness, a list of priorities that would have meaning rather than being demeaning. "I came that they may have life, and have it abundantly."

I heard the echo of these words in a sunlit garden and tasted the possibility of newness there; and, strangely enough, it was in a garden for the blind that my own eyes were opened to something I had not seen very clearly before.

Chapter
14

One of the Landmark Events in our family's career was our discovery of the zip code book. It was surely the most fortunate discovery we made that whole summer.

It all began on a sticky summer night when everyone was tired—and silly. We had gathered around the kitchen table, the only spot in the house where there was some air stirring. We had consumed what must have been gallons of lemonade and an equally appalling quantity of popcorn, and our conversation had disintegrated into a sort of slapstick comedy.

Just how we happened to start talking about zip codes I can't recall. But suddenly the Zip Code Directory was in front of us, and the evening became uproarious.

We discovered Uno, Virginia and Ino, Virginia—but, alas, we couldn't turn up any We-all-know Virginia. However, our disappointment over that was quickly replaced by another burst of merriment when we discovered two towns, quite close together, with names which suggested that their proximity to each other must have been for a valid and urgent reason: Wetmore and Fort Necessity!

How well I recall our glee when we found out that the big state of Texas had a Cheapside!

Some of the names we found that night were almost unbelievable, and we laughed so hard that we finally had to close the book in self-defense.

Our entire family can recall that summer night rather vividly, but little did any of us guess that the evening's laughter was the prelude of a journey that would take me to every state in the Union—at least on paper.

A new world opened up to me out of the zip code book. After our preliminary peregrinations, I grew more and more curious about the origins of the remarkable place names we had come across. Finally I decided that instead of idly wondering about them, I'd write some letters of inquiry to satisfy my curiosity.

Early that fall I sent letters to the postmasters of the two hundred towns which had what I considered to be the most unusual names in the book. I asked each postmaster to share with me the story behind the naming of his town, as well as any other historic information that would be of interest. Then I sat back and waited, hopeful that I might receive at least a few answers.

Before long the replies started coming—two, ten, two dozen, fifty, a hundred, twelve dozen, a hundred and fifty, and, at final count, almost two hundred letters from all over the country!

The stories these letters told were amusing and absorbing, heroic and beautiful, and often profoundly moving. And from every letter I learned something I hadn't known before.

For instance, a woman who had served for over forty years as the postmaster of a Kansas town opened her letter with a lesson that she considered quite elementary. Playfully she chided me for the wording of my salutation:

"Dear Postmaster or Postmistress, as the case may be—"; and she explained, with a twinkle in her pen, "There is no such thing as a postmistress. Whether we are men or women, we are all called postmasters (it would be scandalous, you know, if we were mistresses!)." Then she went on to share with me some intensely interesting facts about her beloved town. And her letter closed with a request for assistance on some of her hobbies, of which she listed fourteen!

The letter that traveled the longest distance was from Chicken, Alaska! The postmaster there explained, with great good humor, that in that part of Alaska the ptarmigan bird has always been very plentiful, but that the old-timers hadn't known how to spell "ptarmigan" so had named their tiny community "Chicken"—which it has been ever since!

The letters that came were informative and inspiring and often contained many bursts of laughter. But they all had one thing in common: a deep pride in the early beginnings of their towns and in the men and women who had given heart and nerve and sinew to make their dreams a reality. There were some magnificent stories of the rugged people who had wrested the little villages from out of the wilderness—scooping them out of the swampland, carving them out of the dense forests, and breathing them into being on the edge of the desert and the windswept plains.

As I read these letters, I discovered that what had begun as an exercise in humor had turned out to be, instead, a highly exciting course in American history! Then, as I thought more carefully about what I had been reading, I couldn't help wondering why we hadn't been teaching history this way in our schools. So much of what our children learn about our country has to do with battles won or lost and the generals who fought them. How much more alive and meaningful our history might become if it were to be taught through the stories of the little towns and the lives of the men and women who built them!

The children growing up today have a general overview of the story of their country, but I would hazard the guess that few of them have much knowledge of the history of their own community; and, likewise, their knowledge of church history is made up primarily of broad, general facts, with the result that the only names they recognize are those belonging to the top echelon of ecclesiastical great. As for the history of the local congregation, there seems to be a great void in most people's thinking, children and adults alike—unless a centennial celebration may have occasioned some research and a reawakened awareness of the past.

This goes back again to the old mountaineer's observation, doesn't it—"Yew cain't give what yew hain't got . . ."

It would be entirely in order to question what connection zip codes and church history could possibly have with one's search for meanings. Simply this: when life is rootless it holds little promise of fruit; and whatever achievement any of us may hope for in the future must be nourished by the past.

So I covet for all of us a thorough knowledge of the people and events that have shaped our lives; and I would hope that each of us might look at that past, not in shadowy outlines, but in the bright colors of individual personalities and specific moments in time—which is why I have taken the time to remember half-forgotten roads and why I am still searching with my family and friends for some valid and enduring landmarks.

To be apathetic about our yesterdays is to be anxious about our tomorrows. To be vague about where we've come from is to be dissatisfied with where we are. To be rootless is to be empty.

All this was stated a long time ago, simply but ever so perceptively, by One who grew up in a very little town. He may not have been the postmaster there, but he was a Master of men. His town never had a zip code, nor will it ever need one, for everyone has heard of Nazareth and the Teacher who lived there—the One who gave us confidence in the past, courage for the present, and hope for the future when he said, "I am the vine, you are the branches."

Chapter
15

Usually we tend to think of landmarks as just what the word suggests: marks on the land—towns, towers, mills, monuments, buildings, bridges, hills, historic houses, spires and cemeteries, and the list could go on. But it has occurred to me that landmarks might also be marks left on the mind; and such "landmarks" would run the entire gamut of human experience.

This type of "landmark of the mind" might be one of those incredible October days when the whole world is bathed in gold, when one heaps high the sum total of his happy moments—like great mounds of extravagant leaves—and tumbles joyously in all the Great Inconsequentials of yesterday.

Such a glorious landmark is an experience that is as vivid to me today as if it had just happened, although it actually took place twenty-six years ago (which would almost put it in the category of Ancient History)!

A friend of mine and I were in New York City to see the stage version of *Peter Pan*. We had built up such a tingling anticipation of our evening at the theater that it

74

was difficult to settle back in our seats when the curtain went up.

The performance exceeded our most extravagant hopes, and I was particularly delighted with the portrayal of Tinker Bell. She was the good fairy who was represented by a twinkly light that flitted here and there across the stage.

In the final scene we watched Tinker Bell move over to a cup of poison that had been intended for Peter Pan and "drink" it in order to save him. Almost immediately the light began to flicker, and the audience realized that Tinker Bell was desperately ill. The light grew dimmer and dimmer. Then, suddenly, Peter Pan sprang to the footlights and addressed the audience:

"Friends, the poison is working swiftly and Tinker Bell is growing very weak. Yet there is still a chance that she can get well—but only you can make it happen. If you want Tinker Bell to live, please applaud."

I looked fleetingly at the sophisticated audience around me, and my heart sank. It was preposterous to think that these people would respond to Peter Pan's request. But I was wrong.

Suddenly the theater rocked with the most thunderous applause I had ever heard! The audience not only clapped, they stood up and cheered and stamped their feet!

Then, bit by bit, the light that had grown so dim began to grow brighter; and soon it started to move, almost imperceptibly at first, then with quicker and stronger movements. And a great shout of rejoicing went up from the audience! Tinker Bell would live!

Tears of joy spilled down my cheeks, and my friend was crying, too. The moment was so touching and so fragile, it seemed to have been made of gossamer.

I have thought of that moment, that magic evening,

many times since, and of that marvelous audience. Underneath all the jewels and the sables and the stiffly starched tuxedo shirts there had been pulsing a longing to believe in goodness and a powerful urge to express love. And, when offered the opportunity for expression, this pent-up emotion had come cascading out of the heart like some magnificent waterfall, unleashing a great wave of joy that inundated everybody there!

How true it is that love cannot be dammed up for long. In time it must find release. But, unhappily, there are many people today who feel so awkward and self-conscious about expressing their concern and their compassion that they keep "holding back." And, like water that has no place to go and so begins to seep out and undermine the walls that have held it back, love that is continually walled in will gradually undermine the very life that has kept it captive.

Probably there is no surer safety valve than the one Christ offered for controlling the floodgates of our lives, allowing for the necessary intervals of storing up and the equally necessary times for pouring out. It is the pouring out that is so difficult. We all become adept at hoarding and saving and storing; but we are hesitant when it comes to opening, relinquishing, giving. But One who lived long ago by a lake called Galilee knew a great deal about water and the way it works; and he has much to teach, too, about the levels of loving of which the human heart is capable.

I may have digressed a long way from Peter Pan and Tinker Bell. But might it not be safe to say that sometimes a flight of fancy is necessary to launch us on a flight of faith?

Chapter
16

Standing at the ironing board or washing the dishes or peeling potatoes or polishing furniture or stirring pudding is a good time to think, and I have been doing a lot of thinking recently.

As a matter of fact, I just prepared a bowl of pudding, and the dessert reminded me of the first pudding my older daughter ever made. I wonder if she still remembers it? More likely she tried to forget the whole thing as quickly as possible.

She was nine or ten years old, I think, and going through that enchanting period of her life when she was always planning surprises.

I had come home from town late one afternoon and was met at the door with a somewhat startling announcement: "Mother, I've made a surprise for you, but I think it's turned out to be more of a surprise than I wanted it to be!"

"Oh?" I asked cautiously, bracing myself for what might follow.

"Well, come into the kitchen and take a look at what I've made."

There on the counter were five dessert dishes, each filled with a nondescript white spongy substance.

"What have you made?" I asked, trying to sound casual and diplomatic.

"It's supposed to be lemon pudding," she replied, with consternation creeping into her voice; "but the trouble is, it doesn't have any lemon flavor!"

I approached the dessert with great trepidation. After taking a taste of it (as small a taste as I felt I could get by with), I had to admit that it had no flavor at all. I was thoroughly puzzled as to what could possibly have gone wrong, for I was certain that she had used a packaged pudding mix.

"Wasn't there a tiny round capsule of lemon flavoring in the package?" I inquired.

She thought hard for a long minute. Then, with a glimmer of understanding in her eyes and a rather sheepish smile, she exclaimed, "Ooooooooh—that's what that was! While I was stirring the pudding, waiting for it to come to a boil, this little thing kept bobbing around. I didn't know what it was; but I figured it was something that had gotten into the package by mistake, so I took it out."

"If you had waited just a little longer," I explained, "the heat of the pudding would have burst the flavor capsule—and then you would have had what you thought you were going to get: lemon pudding!"

"Oh, my goodness," she groaned, "then I threw the flavor out myself!"

Without realizing it, she had coined an appropriate commentary on what many of us do with our lives—we throw the flavor out ourselves and then wonder why the daily round seems so humdrum.

Far-fetched as it may sound, she had given me a new

landmark for finding my way more intelligibly through Paul's second letter to Timothy in which he suggests that we should rekindle, *stir up*, the gift of God within us.

But it takes a considerable bit of stirring, sometimes, before the flavor comes through . . .

Chapter
17

Corners can be both intriguing and irritating. When you're vacuuming a room, it's awkward to get into them; when you're waxing a floor, it's even worse! And when you're papering the walls with a matching design, that's when corners are the worst of all!

Making a bed properly means that there should be snug and well-turned corners; sewing a garment or draperies becomes more exacting when one gets to the corners; and even in the process of baking a cake, one has to pay special attention to the corners of the pan to make sure they are well greased so that the cake won't stick.

I remember how, when my daughters were little, they "helped" their brother construct his awesome structures of Lincoln logs and tinker toys. They learned early how important corners were. For if the corners of the foundations were off kilter, it was not possible to erect anything very stable or very high. And so all three children began spending more time putting their corners in place.

Corners continued to have a part in the children's lives as they grew from year to year. When they first started to school, I often heard them call out to a friend, "I'll race you to the corner!" Then, after they'd grown up a little more, I noticed a change in verbs, and racing to the corner gave way to meeting at the corner.

Fortunately by the time our children began school, punishments didn't include standing in the corner—which is probably why corners never had any unpleasant associations for them during their very early years. But, on the other hand, they didn't have to get through too many birthdays to realize that it was entirely possible to be "backed into a corner," even when there wasn't any actual corner visible.

Then, growing older and wiser, they went through the phase of trying to "cut corners," only to discover that cutting corners generally turned out to be a delusion and that you ended up by taking the longer way around, after all.

Gradually, as they have moved through the teen years, they have learned about the corners of the heart—those cozy places where we tuck some of our warmest memories and experiences. They have been finding out how enjoyable it is to dip into those corners and draw from them the treasures that have been hidden there. Much as a squirrel stores his nuts through the pleasant weather as insurance against the season of leanness, so should we gather up and store the gladness we experience along the way, to tide us over whatever somber season of the heart may lie ahead.

What we pile into the corners of the heart is of paramount importance, for none of us knows what emergency or change in circumstance will make it necessary for us to survive on what we have stored away.

During the Second World War, two women who had been missionaries in China were held in a Communist prison for two hundred days. Writing of their ordeal in a deeply moving book, they referred again and again to the fact that they were able to maintain their sanity because of all the beautiful things they had stored in their minds over the years.

In prison they were not allowed to have any books or paper or pencils. Confined to their tiny cells with nothing to do, they would have found the bleak hours unbearable if they had not been able to fall back on the storehouse of the mind. Over and over they reviewed what they had memorized years before: poems, hymns, Bible verses, the plots of their favorite novels and plays, the names and relationships of friends, the names of places and all the interesting facts that could be recalled about those places. Over and over the women went back to their "memory bank"; and the golden coins of remembrance clinked hopefully against the empty hours, calming the mind and healing the heart.

We should all insist on taking sufficient time to gather together in the corners of our hearts those memories, those ideas, those values that will comprise a sort of "survival kit" if we ever come to a day that seems devoid of sun.

I am only reiterating an idea so old that it was expressed, originally, nearly two thousand years ago: "Do not lay up for yourselves treasures on earth, where moth and rust consume and where thieves break in and steal, but lay up for yourselves treasures in heaven, where neither moth nor rust consumes and where thieves do not break in and steal. For where your treasure is, there will your heart be also." (Matthew 6:19-21)

Chapter
18

Indian summer days seem to have been designed for playing outdoors. The children sense that there will not be many more of these mellow days, when they can be outside without coats and boots and mittens, so they play with added gusto and are more reluctant than usual to go in for supper when they are called.

I could see the neighbors' children at play one such mild, late fall afternoon, while I was sitting in the living room finishing some mending (my husband's coat pockets had reached the three-safety-pin stage again).

The doorbell rang as I was sewing on the last button. It was Ruth stopping by, a friend of mine who is always enthusiastic and effervescent! She dropped in to leave a sampling of a new cookie recipe she had just tried; and, since she wasn't dashing off to another appointment, I put the coffeepot on and we talked. She said she really needed the coffee because she had been awake most of the night before. But, in her ever-cheery way, she commented that although she hadn't been able to sleep, she had had a good time playing hide-and-go-seek in her mind, peeking in all the corners for a particular group of words that she was after.

"Have you ever stopped to consider how many words end in '-ation'?" she asked, with her eyes sparkling mischievously.

"Why, no, I can't say that I have," I replied.

"Well you'd be surprised!" she went on. "There are dozens and dozens of them! In fact, I found so many last night that I finally had to group them in major categories!"

"Give me some examples," I coaxed.

And so she mentioned the general category of life, which is made up of a variety of "-ations": creation, generation, education, vocation, aspiration, motivation, imagination, consideration, temptation, obligation, and celebration!

Then she suggested another broad category—the life of the nation.

"Now help me think of some "-ation" words for that!"

The examples came thick and fast: such words as taxation (frustration!), representation, inauguration, administration, exploration, annexation, conservation, negotiation, segregation, liberation, Emancipation Proclamation, assassination, industrialization, commercialization . . .

Trying to call a halt to our word game was out of the question.

"Let's see how good our concentration is in finding some '-ation' words for the church!" I suggested enthusiastically. And again we were off: revelation, personification, affirmation, reformation, denomination, assimilation, unification, transformation, salvation, and justification.

We paused to take inventory, and we could see almost at once that we had left out several key words, so we added annunciation, purification, sanctification, and reconciliation.

It was a stimulating time of sharing, and we found a great deal to talk about for the rest of the afternoon. Even Ruth was rather surprised at where her night of insomnia had led her! The game of hide-and-go-seek which she had played when sleep eluded her had taken the two of us into many unexpected corners.

The enumer*ation* of all those words suddenly brought us to a realiz*ation* that sometimes something as simple as a game will help us make an evalu*ation* of priorities (it looks as if I can't stop playing!). In pinpointing the "trigger words" in the important areas of our lives, we come face to face with our own value systems.

Now quite apart from the words that end in "-ation," I wonder what sort of list any of us might come up with if we were to jot down what we consider to be the most meaningful words in the New Testament. And if we were to be limited to a list of what we felt were the ten most important, which ten would they be?

Chapter 19

Well, she finally hung up—but the cake baked just a little too long.

She always calls at the very worst times, Mrs. Hoh does. Actually, that isn't her name, but I'll explain that a little later.

If we're having company for dinner and I have only twenty minutes left to change my clothes and set the table, she calls.

If I've just spray-starched the clothes and the iron is just the right temperature, she calls.

When someone's coming by for me in ten minutes and I still have to fix my hair, guess who calls.

If there's a long-distance call coming through momentarily, you know who it is that ties up the phone.

If I'm rolling out a pie crust and I'm up to my elbows in flour, you guessed it . . .

If my hair is all lathered with shampoo and I look and feel like a funny ice-cream sundae—she doesn't phone, she comes!

No matter where you live, you'll find a Mrs. Hoh. She becomes what you secretly think of as a Horrid Old Habit (which is where I first got the idea for her name).

And then it occurred to me that H-O-H also fit the first letters of the words in her favorite conversation openers: "Hang on, Honey, I want to read you something!", or "Hurry over, Honey, I've got the most marvelous bargain to show you!"

So this is how "Mrs. Hoh" came into being.

I've been trying, recently, to find some redemptive value in all of this. Surely Mrs. Hoh's phone calls serve some good purpose, for I have often heard that "there's good in everything—if you look long enough." Heaven knows I've been looking—a long time! At long last, I think I've come up with an idea.

We all need something or someone to keep us humble, else we would soon become insufferably puffy people. It may be a nagging habit that keeps dogging our steps; it might be something physical, like a migraine or acne or even an ulcer; and then, again, it could be a particular person who periodically pops into our lives to jar us just when we're beginning to feel superior and self-sufficient.

Lately I've become not only philosophical about Mrs. Hoh, but even charitable! As a matter of fact, I'm even beginning to think of her, not as a Horrid Old Habit— but as a representative of the Hound of Heaven.

When my life is running smoothly and I feel I know most of the answers, I need an interruption now and then to remind me that my own little schemes and routines aren't infallible. When I begin to feel so self-assured that I think I can "go it alone" without any help from anybody—particularly Anybody—then something needs to be turned topsy-turvy to shake me out of my smugness. And Mrs. Hoh is very good at this.

More and more I am becoming convinced that Mrs. Hoh is a messenger of the Hound of Heaven, because *she* has lived in every town *I've* ever lived in, and she's just around the corner. I simply can't escape her, nor the inexorable discipline of having to rearrange my days or my thinking or my attitudes because of her. Bless her, little does she know how frustrating she is to me—or how much I need her!

And how often I am in need of recalling the lines from Francis Thompson's immortal poem, "The Hound of Heaven":

> I fled Him, down the nights and down the days;
>   I fled Him, down the arches of the years;
> I fled Him, down the labyrinthine ways
>   Of my own mind; and in the mist of tears
> I hid from Him, and under running laughter.
>   Up vistaed hopes I sped;
>   And shot, precipitated,
> Adown Titanic glooms of chasméd fears,
>   From those strong Feet that followed, followed after

Chapter
20

Our two old washtubs were sold at the rummage sale today. Actually, I had rather mixed feelings when they went. On the one hand, I was glad to get rid of them, because they'd been taking up so much space; but, on the other hand, there was such a lot of nostalgia in those tubs that I felt as if I were saying good-bye to two old friends.

Those two tubs could tell many stories, I'm sure; but perhaps the one that they would choose to tell would be the same one Candace and I would select. Or maybe she was too young when this happened, to recall it—although she had pattered down to the basement after me that particular washday, and witnessed the little drama which I lifted her up to see.

I had gone down to do an emergency load of washing in the afternoon. As I lifted the hose to fill the first rinse tub, I noticed a box-elder bug struggling upside down in a groove at the bottom of the tub. There was a little bit of water in the groove, left over from the morning washing, and somehow the little hard-shelled bug had gotten into the awkward predicament of being flat on its back and flailing its legs in an effort to get right side up again.

Not being inordinately fond of box-elder bugs, I was about to train the hose on the groove and wash the culprit down the drain. But I paused for a moment to see whether or not the bug might be able to flip itself over onto its legs. As I hesitated, suddenly there appeared from out of nowhere a second box-elder bug. It made its way diagonally across the bottom of the tub, over to the groove where the other bug was still struggling.

What happened next was so surprising that, even after seeing it, I could scarcely believe what I'd seen. The box-elder bug that had just arrived on the scene crawled down into the groove, into the residual water, and maneuvered itself underneath the bug that was struggling on its back. With all the might and main of which a little bug would be capable, the "rescuer bug" lifted the first bug up out of the groove and flipped it right side up!

I lifted Candace up so she could watch what took place, and she was as delighted with the drama as I, even though she was too young at the time to have known that we had just witnessed the Story of the Good Samaritan. It had been acted out on a most unlikely stage and by the least likely "actors" that could possibly have been found anywhere! And yet, there it was, the concern and effort expended to help a hapless fellow-being!

I stood and marveled at what I had just seen. Obviously it was unthinkable to wash the bugs down the drain; so I found a piece of cardboard and lifted the two little bugs out of the rinse tub and carried them out into the garden where I could set them free.

The remainder of the afternoon was spent thinking about what had taken place. What was it that had prompted the one bug to come to the aid of the other?

Surely a box-elder bug wasn't large enough to have a brain, and I was even less sure about what sort of heart it could possibly have in so small a body; but there was some remarkable built-in instinct that had made the second bug respond to the plight of its "brother."

We are given so many opportunities to be of service, to be the good Samaritan: to risk, to lift, to bless. Yet, over and over again we turn away, because there is water where we must go and we don't want to get our feet wet. And so we pass by on the other side.

I hope, maybe, my daughter will recall the incident of the box-elder bugs after reviewing the details again. And in remembering, I hope she may find it easier, when she is called upon, to take the role of the Good Samaritan— and risk and lift and bless!

Funny how a rummage sale brings out so many things we had almost forgotten from the far corners of yester-day . . .

Chapter
21

I wish one of my children would get out the guitar and see what might be done to find some chords to accompany a few verses I jotted down after attending a study session on the Book of Jonah. I hadn't read this particular story for years and consequently hadn't remembered any of the details or the significance of that Old Testament narrative and so the refresher course was both stimulating and enjoyable.

After coming home, it occurred to me that there were several books of the Old Testament with which I was totally unfamiliar. Obadiah, Habakkuk, Zephaniah, Joel —had I ever read these? I couldn't be sure, since there didn't seem to be anything I could recall from any of those books. No doubt if I ever had read them, the reading had been done as a "have to" assignment and had apparently meant little to me at the time.

Having had my thinking jogged by the Jonah story, I decided to peruse some of the other books that I had slighted. And it has been a satisfying venture, delving into these books for myself, not because I had to meet a

Course Requirement, but because I really wanted to, for my own interest.

Perhaps this is the fine line between education and learning—the former is usually something prescribed, something you take because you know you're going to need it; the latter is something preferred, an area of knowledge you select for yourself because you genuinely desire it.

So I have launched upon a learning process and am having a very good time exploring the seldom-visited corners of the Old Testament. With a good Commentary as my sextant, I am charting my own course, taking my time—weighing anchor or dropping it, as I wish, and sailing into all the little coves and inlets. And all the time I keep discovering more of the shoreline of my faith. As I view the general topography, I can see how much more there is to explore—also how fragile has been the vessel of my faith. I think this new awareness of incompleteness is what prompted the writing of the verses which follow:

> Noah had a rainbow,
> He even had an ark;
> Why, then, must *I* be content
> To whistle in the dark?
>
> Moses had God's ten commands;
> He had the Red Sea, too—
> Oh, why should I, a child of God,
> Keep merely muddling through?
>
> Daniel had his lion's den;
> Shadrack had a fire;
> Why do I allow myself
> To bog down in this mire?
>
> David overcame Goliath;
> Joshua won his fight—

I just seem to shadowbox
Or else I'm put to flight.

Jonah went to Nineveh,
Not by rail, but whale—
I'm still buffeting about
With every little gale.

Paul had his Damascus Road;
The disciples—loaves and fishes;
Oh, why should I keep clinging to
A few small, flimsy wishes?

Thomas finally lost his doubt;
Magdalene was forgiven—
I've been clearly shown the way,
And yet I'm skirting heaven!

There—it's not much as poetry, and it's even less as theology; but perhaps we can call it, simply, "Confession of a Contrite Christian." What it lacks in cadence perhaps my children can correct with the music they create.

Chapter 22

In the journeying of the years, I find that The Road often leads, not so much through the valley of the shadow of death, but more frequently through the valley of the shadow of doubt. Nevertheless, when the shadows seem the longest, some familiar landmarks loom up on the road ahead of me, and I step forward once again with a confident faith. For true it is, as the line from the beloved hymn reminds us, ". . . gladness breaks like morning where'er Thy face appears!"

Living as they are on the edge of the unexpected, my children—all children—need, more than ever, the sustaining assurance of a heritage that is believable and prideworthy. Coupled with such a heritage must be the kind of courage that Christ's Way provides, a depth of courage that will enable the seeker to look in *all* the corners.

If I am honest with myself (and this is surely one of the most difficult of all disciplines, because it is so easy to make excuses), I shall have to confess that The Road becomes blurred and the landmarks fuzzy only when I permit myself to panic—when I read only the screaming headlines in the newspaper and neglect to read the proclamation of the Good News; when I see only the sorry, sordid side of society and fail to see the shining compassion of his face.

My daughter has asked me to change pace—and I cannot help feeling that all of us would find it easier to walk The Road if we could break ranks with the pessimistic hawkers of doom and fall into step, instead, with the One whose purposeful pace led into the way of peace.

From Capernaum to California to Calcutta, there are corners to turn, corners to explore—and corners to brighten. From Gethsemane to the Gobi Desert to Guadalajara there is grief to lift and grace to offer. From Damascus to Dublin to Detroit there is a Design to discover and to include in the development of our dreams.

So it is that The Road beckons to every generation, promising hope in the second mile. The orthogenesis of hate cannot go beyond the second mile; but the first mile is the longest, and none of us can escape it. But at the corners of our lives stands One who waits to walk that difficult first mile with us. This I must believe; this I *will* believe. And this belief I will offer to my children as they search every corner for meanings and as they find and follow The Road that leads to life and hope and joy.